PRAISE FOR
THINK LIKE A PLANNER

"Melissa and I worked together for many years as part of the same event team. As someone who intimately understands the event planning process, I have seen first-hand Melissa's ability to implement seamless events. She thinks of the big picture and addresses the details. She leaves no stone unturned. If there is someone who can help you develop a plan and provide the encouragement to get there, it's Melissa!"

Angela Hoban, Director, Strategic University Events, Temple University, Philadelphia, PA

"Melissa brings a much-needed skill set to creative thinkers in need of assistance with organization and staying on task. Her step-by-step approach is simple and easy to follow, which is much appreciated. One of the things I love most about working with Melissa is her positive energy. Not only does she provide effective strategies, but she also provides unique insights and encouragement to help you stay motivated along the way."

Dawn Mazzone, Founder, Creative Economy Enterprises, West Chester, PA

"*Think Like a Planner* is a must-read for those of us juggling multiple responsibilities and managing a busy life. Melissa cuts through the everyday distractions that hold us back and helps us develop a plan to reset our focus on what really matters and accomplish our goals. There are many business books that address the planning process if you are a planner, but none are written by a planner for everyday life. Brilliant!"

Lisa Fellman, Founder, Enterprise Marketing & Communications, Voorhees, NJ

"Melissa has always been a planner at heart and has used her organizational abilities throughout her life to plan and implement all kinds of events, including girls' trips, special events, and gatherings. As someone who has known Melissa since kindergarten, I can confirm her true passion for helping others achieve greater success. Her guidance is so applicable to everyday life. I'm so excited to see Melissa share her wealth of experience and skill set with others!"

Melinda Yurick, Reading Specialist and Educator, Lifelong Friend, Bethlehem, PA

"I worked with Melissa on a project that was near and dear to my heart—a book of memories and photographs of my dad who passed away when I was 19. I had always dreamed of creating a book that I could enjoy and share with other family members, especially the seven grandsons my dad never got to meet. Melissa made it happen. Priceless!"

Cindee Saska, Neighbor and Friend, Lakeville, PA

THINK LIKE A PLANNER

Simple Strategies to Stay on Task and Accomplish Your Goals

Melissa G. DelMonego

atmosphere press

Published by Atmosphere Press

Cover design by Felipe Betim

Atmospherepress.com

This book is dedicated to my parents, who gave me the
gifts of love, security, and a positive outlook and my
family and friends, who have inspired me to be a better
person, supported me in this life journey, and with whom
I have shared so many wonderful memories—no words
can express my gratitude.

TABLE OF CONTENTS

INTRODUCTION

Have you set goals that you haven't accomplished?

Do you struggle with staying on task?

Would you like to learn some powerful, yet simple tools to increase your focus, create a plan, and make things happen?

If you answer yes to any of these questions, this book is for you.

In this practical guide, I share strategies and insights I have used effectively in my thirty-year event planning career and help you apply them in your daily life to be more successful.

Whether you are...

> ➤ In need of fresh perspectives to jump-start your productivity;
>
> ➤ Overwhelmed by day-to-day responsibilities and would like to maintain more focus;
>
> ➤ Frustrated by juggling multiple tasks and seeking more balance; or
>
> ➤ Interested in creating a healthy and productive routine.

...creating a plan and staying on task are essential for success. And that's exactly what this book delivers: easily applied strategies to think differently, create your own unique plan of action, and set yourself up for success.

➤ You'll be more organized with a vision of what you want to accomplish and a road map for getting there.

➤ You'll be able to set boundaries, focus, and be more productive.

➤ You'll feel less frustrated and more empowered and energized by the momentum behind your actions.

➤ And you'll have the skills to regroup if you find yourself getting off track in the future.

Because I appreciate the value of time and truly believe in using time to its fullest potential, here are the benefits you can expect from the time you invest in reading this book:

➤ **Six Specific Strategies** that you can use to stay on task and increase productivity in your daily life.

➤ **Exercises** that help you apply the information learned.

➤ **A Simple-to-Follow Worksheet** that you can use to get started immediately.

Please know that change in general is not easy for anyone. But it can be done. It just takes some tools, a plan, and encouragement. And that's what this book provides. Let's get started!

THE POWER
OF FOCUS

***

"In a world filled with distraction, attention is our competitive advantage."

– Jocelyn K. Glei

***

LET'S BEGIN WITH FOCUS. What is focus and why is it so important to drive plans forward and make things happen?

Focus is defined by Webster's Dictionary as "to concentrate attention or effort on some<u>thing</u>." Notice how this definition includes ONE thing, not "things." Focus is one of the key habits of highly successful people. It is the ability to concentrate on <u>one</u> thing at a time and do it well. There is power in focusing on one thing at a time and giving it your full attention. I know a lot of people who use the term "multitasking" to describe what they can do. But I think that term is misleading. I don't think that human beings can be successful if our attention is spread across too many areas at one time. It's just not humanly possible.

In fact, according to Dr. Christian Jarrett, psychologist and author of *The Rough Guide to Psychology*, studies have shown that the human mind can only truly multitask when it comes to highly automatic behaviors like walking. But for activities that require conscious attention, there really is no such thing as multitasking, only task-switching. I think this makes sense if we really think about it—we call it multitasking, but what we are really doing is switching from task to task. There is no way we can focus on a television show AND follow a recipe AND have a meaningful conversation with another human being and do all these tasks well at the same time. The quality of all these tasks will suffer. And not only will the quality of the tasks suffer, but activities will take longer to complete than they normally would if a single task had been the sole focus. The reason is that trying to do more than one thing at a time breaks our concentration and, therefore, our ability to focus. Also, not being able to complete a task keeps that task in our minds and keeps us from focusing on other tasks. This creates a distraction, one of the key inhibitors to accomplishing our goals.

I have experienced this in my own life. If I have too many things going on at once or too many thoughts in my head at once, I am not able to focus or concentrate on the task at hand. I walk in circles, thinking about what to do next. And if I am working on a task too late into the evening and don't complete it, I can't sleep because my mind is racing thinking about that task.

This is why it is important to focus on one task at a time and finish it or find a good stopping point—one that frees your mind from nagging questions—before moving on. If we can learn to focus and concentrate our efforts, we can be more productive and use our focus to our advantage. I truly believe that the ability to focus is a game changer and can help you address your struggles, be more successful, and even set yourself apart.

So, let's begin with looking at what holds you back from being able to focus. Is it...

➢ Too many commitments?

➢ Feeling overwhelmed?

➢ Feeling unorganized?

➢ Too many distractions?

➢ Trying to multitask?

➢ Fear of failure?

All these reasons are valid. We all can get distracted by life's requests and feel overwhelmed and disorganized at times, no doubt. Many of us wear multiple hats and are torn in different directions. We manage our own personal schedules such as appointments, interests, and work; family schedules such as school activities and bedtime routines; home responsibilities such as meal planning, house cleaning, and home repairs;

and sometimes aging parents. As a result, our own needs can be pushed aside. We don't have an issue with any of these responsibilities. It's just hard to find balance and focus.

Take a moment now to check in with yourself and list the **top three (3) obstacles** that are holding you back, things that come to mind almost without thinking.

What is holding me back?

1.

2.

3.

In my case, I am of the "sandwich generation," the "caught-in-the-middle" generation raising children and taking care of older parents, each with their own set of physical and emotional needs that makes it very stressful and time-consuming. My son is soon to be 21, living in Colorado, exploring possibilities and what he wants to do in life, and my mother will be 95 and has overcome some serious health issues, but is resilient and strong. My priority is to be available to my son when he needs guidance and someone to listen, but I also need to be available for my mother as I am her advocate and only support. These activities, while super important, are time-consuming, sometimes stressful, and make it more difficult to focus on accomplishing personal goals like developing a consistent nutrition and exercise plan or writing this book.

Let's face it—this is life, right? We can't just walk away from responsibilities and only focus on ourselves. That is not realistic. But it is important that we find ways to keep a positive perspective and stay organized and empowered so that we don't lose sight of ourselves or our goals. After all, our health and well-being are critically important to our family's well-being. Using some simple strategies can help us navigate our day more effectively and achieve greater success. And recognizing what is happening is half of the battle.

I have found the following **six (6) strategies** to be extremely useful in helping me to focus, stay on task, and achieve my goals. I'm sharing them with you because I want you to be successful too.

STRATEGY 1

Visualize Success

"Through visualization, you can turn an abstract hope into a picture that not only inspires you, but also guides you."

– Deepak Chopra

THE TOPIC OF VISUALIZATION is so interesting to me because I am a visual learner and I think many of us are. Visualization may seem like a hard-to-grasp concept and some may question its benefits. But in fact, research has shown that there is a strong scientific basis for how and why visualization works.

A fascinating Blog in HuffPost, formerly the Huffington Post, by Srinivasan Pillay, CEO of NeuroBusiness Group and award-winning author, explains how it is now a well-known fact that we stimulate the same brain regions when we visualize an action and when we actually perform that same action. For example, when you visualize lifting your right hand, it stimulates the same part of the brain that is activated when you actually lift your right hand. This shared area of brain activation when we imagine an action and perform it has been demonstrated extensively in scientific literature.

A striking example of how visualization increases brain activation is seen in stroke cases. When a person has a stroke due to a blood clot in a brain artery, blood cannot reach the tissue that the artery once fed with oxygen and nutrients, and that tissue dies. This tissue death then spreads to the surrounding area that does not receive the blood anymore. However, if a person with this stroke imagines moving the affected arm or leg, brain blood flow to the affected area increases and the surrounding brain tissue is saved. Imagining moving a limb, even after it has been paralyzed due to a stroke, increases brain blood flow enough to diminish the amount of tissue death. This is a very strong indicator of the power of visualization.

There are many examples of how athletes have used the practice of visualization for a very long time to improve performance, including preparing for the Olympics. They envisage themselves successfully completing the task, seeing themselves in a victory situation. Some athletes prefer to use the term "imagery vs. visualization" because it involves all senses and is more of an all-encompassing experience.

But what is happening during this process? One is rewiring one's brain through a process called neuroplasticity, which is the ability of neural networks in the brain to change through growth and reorganization. It is when the brain is rewired to function in some way that differs from how it previously functioned. Visualization is one tool that can help you engage this process and retrain your brain.

Dr. Sanja Gupta, a neurosurgeon, journalist, and professor at Emory University's School of Medicine, explains that "just by changing your thoughts, you can modulate your heart rate, blood pressure, and immune system. That said, if you want to be a high achiever, you must train your brain to think in a way that sets you up for success."

Visualization, like other techniques that can rewire your brain, such as meditation and mindfulness, takes focus and practice. As with any new habit you want to create, it takes time. How long it takes will depend upon the person and the situation. According to James Clear, author of the #1 New York Times bestseller, *Atomic Habits*, we should be realistic in setting our expectations appropriately because the truth is, it could take anywhere from two to eight months to adopt a new behavior. But you can't reach your goal if you don't begin. I think James provides some wise advice: "At the end of the day, how long it takes to form a particular habit doesn't really matter that much. Whether it takes 50 days or 500 days, you have to put in the work either way. The only way to get to Day 500 is to start with Day 1. So, forget about the number and focus on doing the work."

I have used visualization and brain re-training in my own life when I have wanted to change my behavior and have experienced positive results.

➢ I have used visualization to build my confidence in trying more difficult ski trails by creating an image of myself skiing them successfully.

➢ I have used visualization to change my eating habits and lose weight by visualizing a healthier me, which directly impacted my food choices.

➢ I have used visualization to evaluate and make job changes early in my career.

➢ I have used visualization to write this book by seeing the end product in my hands and the happiness felt from sharing expertise and helping others succeed.

You can use this technique in any number of ways throughout your life to create change. It is amazing how the practice of visualization can enable the brain to be retrained to achieve a specific outcome. To me, it's a very exciting topic as I believe we have only scratched the surface of what is possible related to brain training through practices such as visualization, meditation, and mindfulness.

So why is visualization important to goal setting?

Well, to accomplish your goals, it is important for you to imagine what you want to accomplish and, just as importantly, who you want to be once you accomplish your goals. Imagining who you want to be, in addition to what you want to accomplish, creates a stronger connection between action and accomplishment. You create a picture in your mind, something concrete that can guide you.

One of the ways we can visualize our goals is by writing them down. Writing things down creates visualization and intention or commitment. And commitment is needed to accomplish your goals. You can't do it any other way. You need to be laser-focused on the goals you write down. Anything that doesn't support those goals gets put aside. Writing down your goals makes them real and proclaims to yourself and others with whom you share them that this is how you will spend your time, that these actions are important to you, and that you are committed to accomplishing them. Writing down your goals also creates a visual of them in your mind and helps you focus. By visualizing your goals daily, you are cementing them in your thinking and setting yourself up for success.

So, write down your goals, commit them to paper, and post them where you can see them daily. Visualize them. Anything that doesn't support these goals, let it go.

Some of you may be asking, "But how do I identify my goals?" If you need assistance with this, the following exercise will be extremely beneficial. We'll explore each of these areas in greater detail below.

1. Identify Core Values

Identify the things that are most important to you; the things that you value. You will be more successful if your goals align with your values because they'll be synchronized with who you are as a person and what you deem to be important. Understanding your core values will help you to stay on task and reset your direction when times get tough or life becomes overwhelming. You will be able to remind yourself why you have chosen your goals and the path you are pursuing. Knowing your core values will also help you establish a daily structure, something I address in Chapter 3. There are so many things in life pulling us in so many different directions that we must focus or risk getting nothing done at all.

2. Identify Goals

Make a list of things you'd like to accomplish. Be specific. Review how this list aligns with your core values. Be realistic. And think about how you want to spend your time. Remember, your time is limited, so with the limited time that you have, what do you want to accomplish?

3. Set a Target Time Frame for Each Goal

Set a time frame for each goal. Be realistic. A key strategy that planners use is "working backward." This strategy, discussed in Chapter 5, comes in handy when creating a task list and mapping out a plan for accomplishing your goals.

4. Create a Visual Plan

P.L.A.N. (Personal List of Actions Now)

Once you have identified your values and goals and given thought to time frames, use the template provided below to develop a plan that you can print and look at daily to stay on task.

Core Values Exercise

You may not realize it, but your core values—those things in which you strongly believe and are non-negotiable—drive your actions almost without thinking. These values have been created through your life experiences and through any self-awareness you have used to change or modify your actions. They drive your life decisions, including the products you use, the people and companies you support, and how and with whom you spend your time. When you go against your core values, it can lead to stress and frustration. Therefore, it is essential that you understand what drives you and use this information to set yourself up for success.

To identify your core values, spend some time thinking about the things that identify you as a person and provide guidance for your actions. This may come naturally or may be something you have not thought about before. There are many references for identifying values. I have found Brene Brown's *List of Values* to be particularly helpful. Once you have identified a values list, simply refer to the list and identify the **five (5) values** that describe or resonate with you the most. You can certainly go beyond five, but the purpose of this exercise is to zone in on those values you deem most important. As you do this, think about the things that you couldn't live without. Also, think about the decisions you have made thus far: when you have felt positive and when you have felt frustrated. Positive feelings are generated when decisions are in line with core values. If you are struggling, ask others in your life which values they would select for you. This may give you some interesting insights to consider.

As an example, some of the core values that I have identified in my own life include:

Health & Wellness

Being healthy directly impacts my quality of life and my ability to enjoy activities with my family such as traveling, hiking, and skiing. I want to be able to participate in as many activities as possible for as long as possible, so I make it a priority to carve out time during my day for exercise and try to maintain a healthy diet, which includes drinking plenty of water. Being healthy also includes emotional well-being, so I try to schedule time for things that bring me joy and rejuvenation when I am able, such as gardening. I also stay on top of medical appointments and screenings. I know this is one of my core values because when I look back on my life, a focus on health and wellness has always been present.

Integrity

It has always been important to me to be true to myself and live life in alignment with my beliefs and convictions. To do what I say and say what I do. To follow through on commitments. I think this was an example set by my parents as I was growing up without my full awareness at the time. But because I grew up with a strong sense of integrity, when I am asked to do something that is not in alignment with this value, I feel a strong visceral response that brings about stress and anxiety and I know I am out of alignment with one of my core values.

Relationships

I can see how important this core value is to me in how I have cultivated and maintained relationships throughout my life such as those with my loving family as well as the many friends

I have met through high school, college, the working world, and since becoming a parent. I am still close with friends I met in kindergarten. I cherish each and every one of my friends and family members and the love and meaning they bring to my life.

Gratitude

Having a sense of gratitude helps me keep a positive perspective in life. It helps me respond to life's curveballs with grace and humility. It makes me mindful of what is truly important. And it fuels my interest in giving back to others, one of my main reasons for writing this book. I want to be a source of positivity and encouragement in this world, and gratitude is key to that endeavor.

Creativity

One of the things I most enjoy is organizing thoughts and images into memory books, calendars, and gifts. It is the combination of organizing the material and marrying it with pictures to tell a story that brings me joy. I can tell I am in alignment with this core value when I am creating as I am full of endless energy and excitement and can lose track of time.

Hopefully these examples have helped you understand a bit more about the importance of core values in your life and how you might recognize them in your daily actions. Now, refer to the values list you have identified and list the **five (5) values** that describe or resonate with you the most.

Core Values Exercise Template

My five (5) core values. Feel free to add more if necessary.

1.

2.

3.

4.

5.

Goals Exercise

Goals should support your values and be specific and time-driven in that they should have a start and end date. Goals don't need to relate to just one aspect of your life. You might have travel goals and professional goals and financial goals and health & wellness goals. Goals can relate to any aspect of your life in which you want to accomplish something. And you might have many goals that you want to accomplish over time. That's okay. I have many interests and goals I want to accomplish too. Some are more involved and time-consuming than others. In general, I find that focusing on up to three goals at a time is manageable with my busy schedule.

Here is an example of a well-written, specific, and targeted goal:

Goal: *Exercise for 30-60 minutes 4 times per week.*
Time Frame: *Beginning on Monday, 1/23/23. Ongoing.*

This goal supports one of my core values noted previously: staying healthy. It is specific in that it outlines the tasks I need to accomplish. And it is time-driven with a start date. In this case, this goal is ongoing as exercise is really a lifelong activity.

Here is an example of another one of my goals, quite different from the one above:

Goal: *Donate to 6 organizations that support my beliefs and are within my budget in the next 12 months.*
Time Frame: *January 2024 – December 2024*

This goal supports my core value of integrity. It enables me to live with integrity by giving back to things I believe in. The goal is specific as I am searching for six organizations, and it is time-driven in that it focuses on a twelve-month period.

And finally, this last goal example, which relates to planning a special event or celebration:

> **Goal:** *Plan my husband's 2025 60th birthday celebration.*
> *Identify the location and key activities along with places to stay.*
> **Time Frame:** *January 2024 – May 2024*

This goal supports my core value of relationships. I've given myself a specific range of dates and a list of tasks to get started, activities that may need to be reserved well in advance.

Take a moment now to give thought to your goals and assign a time frame for each.

Goals Exercise Template

Identify three (3) goals & time frames.

Goal:

Time Frame:

Goal:

Time Frame:

Goal:

Time Frame:

A word here about time frames. Time frames are necessary to drive plans forward. But sometimes we drive things and sometimes things drive us. Don't beat yourself up. This is life. Be ready to "Roll with the Changes" as REO Speedwagon says, for those of you who know that band. The tools I provide in the rest of this book will help you stay on task. Just continue to move yourself forward and stay focused and you will be successful.

Create a Visual Plan

Use the following template and the information you developed to create a visual plan. Print it out and post it where you can see it daily as a reminder of what you deem most important and what you intend to accomplish.

Visual Plan Example

GOALS	VALUE	TIME FRAME
Exercise for 30-60 minutes four times per week.	Health & Wellness	Beginning on Monday, January 1, 2023. Ongoing
Plan my husband's 60th birthday celebration.	Relationships	January 2024 – May 2024
Donate to 6 organizations that support my beliefs and are within my budget in the next 12 months.	Integrity	January 2024 – December 2024

Visual Plan Template

GOALS	VALUE	TIME FRAME

Keep in mind that this is not a complete list of everything you will be doing in your day-to-day life. There are daily responsibilities that you must tend to, plan for, and allocate time toward, such as meal planning and preparation, taking your children to and from school, your job, etc. Those responsibilities will always take priority. This is a list of things you want to accomplish OUTSIDE of day-to-day responsibilities, which is why staying organized and focused is so important.

This exercise gave you the ability to identify the goals you want to accomplish. It gave you ONE visual to put in front of you every day to stay focused. Great job!

Now let's look at how to **eliminate "noise" and obstacles**—the things that keep us from accomplishing our goals.

STRATEGY 2

Overcome Obstacles

---

*"Obstacles don't have to stop you. If you run into a wall,
don't turn around and give up. Figure out how to climb it,
go through it, or work around it."*

– Michael Jordan

I'LL BE HONEST. I think this strategy is hard, especially in today's world, which is why if we can identify and eliminate many of the distractions that come our way, it will be tremendously helpful in accomplishing our goals. It's hard to completely eliminate all distractions, but even doing just one or two things can make a big difference. The point is, you need to take control to the best of your ability and put a plan into action.

Did you know that it takes an average of about 23 minutes and 15 seconds to return to the original task after an interruption, according to Gloria Mark, who studies digital distraction at the University of California, Irvine? That means that when you get distracted, even for a few minutes, you lose approximately half an hour of productivity. Each time.

So, how do we identify and remove noise and obstacles? Well, we must take some time and think about things that are getting us sidetracked and identify ways to eliminate them or work around them.

➤ Maybe it's someone who is not particularly supportive. Find someone who IS supportive so that you have a positive influence in your life.

➤ Maybe it's someone who interrupts you when you are trying to focus on a task. Simply communicating that you are going to be working on a project for the next hour and would appreciate no interruptions would be helpful to both parties involved.

➢ Maybe your inbox is overwhelming, like mine. Decide to check emails at certain times during the day so you don't get sidetracked. Turn off your email pop-up notification so you don't get distracted. And unsubscribe from emails you don't need.

➢ Maybe you need to create your own quiet, uninterrupted space where you can go to create. If there is noise around you and it is difficult to focus, try listening to inspiring music. This is what I do when I write. Hans Zimmer, who I learned about through my son, is one of my favorite artists. His music is incredibly inspiring and motivational to me.

➢ Maybe you have too many daily responsibilities and it's making it impossible to carve out time for anything else. Ask someone for help. I realized as I was doing my own self-reflection that if I just asked for help, something as simple as once a week—others in my household to be responsible for meals and cleanup, for instance—I could take back 4-6 hours of time for myself to focus on my goals. Because I am a "doer" by nature, I do not think to ask for help. If I want something done, I just do it. But that is not helping me accomplish my goals. Asking for help...so simple, yet so powerful. Don't be afraid to ask for help.

The bottom line is that to be successful, you need to take charge of your time and be in control of what goes into your plan. Don't be afraid to say no. Warren Buffet has said, *"The difference between successful people and very successful people is that very successful people say 'no' to almost everything."*

I realize that this is easier said than done. Many tasks that occur daily can't be declined. When a family member gets sick or has an emergency, I can't say "no." When my manager requests my assistance with a presentation or project, I can't say "no." When tasks are due for an upcoming event, I can't say "no." Maybe you had a game plan for the day and the daycare center just called to inform you that your child is sick. Best laid plans! Sometimes we have control and sometimes we just don't. That's okay—that's life. As we work through all six strategies, you'll learn how to keep track of where you left off and how to re-engage when the time is right. Just do your best and little by little you will move forward and accomplish your goals.

For now, look at what is being presented to you and if it doesn't support one of your goals, let it go. Simply say, "This activity doesn't support my goals and my time is limited so I can't participate." There will be time in the future to come back to those things and determine if they are still relevant. For now, let's focus on the goals you have in front of you.

Obstacle Exercise

Identify three (3) things that create distraction and ways to let them go. Add more if necessary.

Obstacle Exercise Example

OBSTACLE	RESOLUTION
1. No quiet time to focus.	Identify a 30–60-minute time block each day, find a space where I can be by myself, and notify others around me that this is my "planning time" and not to disturb me unless it is an emergency.
2. Need to create more "me" time in my day.	Identify an activity, such as cooking a meal, walking the dog, or grocery shopping, that can be delegated to someone else in the household and ask for help in taking over that responsibility one or more days per week.
3. Too many emails in my inbox—looks and feels over-whelming.	Make it a point to unsubscribe immediately to any email that is not required or that I have not requested. Select and delete emails once per week.
4. Too many inter-ests/things I'd like to do.	Practice using this statement: "I'm sorry, but this activity doesn't support my goals at this time and my time is limited so I can't par-ticipate." Put the activity on a list that I can revisit after I accomplish my current goals.

Obstacle Exercise Template

OBSTACLE	RESOLUTION
1.	
2.	
3.	
4.	
5.	

I'll give you some examples of things that have happened to me that required me to let go so I could focus on my goals.

I love to garden. I love to be outdoors and see something that I've planted and nurtured come to life. I had the opportunity to participate in a community garden about five minutes from my house. I thought this would be a great opportunity to grow my own food, share the experience with my young son, spend time with friends, and enjoy nature. Perfect! It supported my goals at the time and was something I had wanted to experience and accomplish. It was great initially until the weeds started to grow, the weather became hot and dry, and the garden became a burden and a place where I HAD to be vs. WANTED to be. I'm a big believer in things happening for a reason and one morning, as I was working in my garden and feeling stressed out, a fellow gardener said something very freeing as I shared my conflicted feelings about the garden. She said, "This just isn't the right season for you to have a garden." She explained that she was retired, and gardening was something she enjoyed in her free time. Trying to have a garden and work and raise a family was just too much for me. I had taken on more than I could do well, and I had to let go. She made me realize that it is okay to say no. I still would like to have a garden or work in a garden someday, but that day is not now. For now, I take care of the flower beds in my yard, which brings me much joy and is much easier to manage.

I also have an interest in tracing my genealogy and have had this interest for some time. I have a goal of someday traveling to places where my ancestors originated and learning more about their history and background. I think this would be an exciting way to add more interest to a family vacation. And although it doesn't sound like it would take much time to gather this input, all actions take time. I decided that until I completed other goals on my list, this activity would need to be placed on hold. What I am trying to do in the meantime is organize family photos and ensure I have names of relatives while family members are still living. This will help me down the road when I am ready to take on this activity.

Finally, I have wanted to write this book and share my organization and planning expertise with others for some time, but life was telling me it just wasn't the right moment. Just when I thought things were in a groove and I could carve out some time for myself, something would happen that swallowed up that extra time. The world was saying no. I had to listen. There were only so many hours in the day and at the end of my day, I was exhausted.

Having said all of this, there will be situations that happen in life that present themselves and are important but do sidetrack us from our day-to-day plan. It is important to recognize and take advantage of these special opportunities. Examples might be a lifelong friend who contacts you and wants to get together or someone who has extra tickets to a special event and asks you to go along. The key is to learn how to absorb these opportunities, regroup, and get back on track.

Next, **creating a daily structure** will be central to setting yourself up for success by understanding what works for you and building your confidence.

STRATEGY 3

Create a Routine

"We are what we repeatedly do."

— Aristotle

RESEARCH SHOWS THAT HUMANS need organization or structure to function well. Even those in creative careers have some structure as to how they create. You can call it structure or routine, but defining a daily pattern is essential to success. And it starts in the morning when you first wake up.

What is the definition of routine? The practice of regularly doing things in a fixed order that requires little conscious thought.

Benefits of a Routine:

➢ Starts your day off in a positive direction. Makes you feel more confident. Gives you a sense of control and power.

➢ Allows you to maximize your time, and better time management leads to greater creativity and productivity.

➢ Allows you to take advantage of your strengths.

➢ Helps you focus by knowing you have a plan and don't need to think or make decisions. It's easier to avoid the noise and distractions.

➢ Reduces your stress by creating a sense of order and calm.

Think about the Earth and life's ecosystems. There is a structure or routine to all that happens: to the way the planets orbit the sun, to wildlife migration patterns, to body biorhythms, to the ebb and flow of tides. There is a reason and a purpose to these systems and humans are part of that plan. I believe that if we develop patterns that are in sync with our natural rhythms, it will lead to greater success. Whatever the pattern, it should be unique to each of us to be successful.

For instance, certain times of the day may be more productive for you. Use those times to focus on things that require the most energy. As an example, I usually tackle tedious tasks mid-morning. That is when I find I am most awake and focused. However, I am not an early riser. I cannot push myself to rise at 6:00 or 7:00 am (or earlier) and expect to be productive. Believe me, I've tried. I can do this on occasion—for instance, if I am traveling and need to be up early for a flight or if I have an early morning appointment—but I cannot do this routinely. And my body rhythm has changed over time as well. Listen to what your body is telling you, and don't fight it. When my son was in school and I had to be up early to take him to school, I had no choice. But then I went to bed early to ensure I got enough sleep. Again, life isn't perfect, and having a plan doesn't mean being inflexible. It just means being aware, listening to what your body is telling you, and doing your best to stay in a groove.

Setting up a routine is like creating a new habit. It takes some time (about 66 days, as we have learned) to establish a pattern. The key is to again give thought to who you are as a person, what makes you tick, and what time of day you are most productive, least productive, most creative, most energetic, etc. This information will be key to designing a routine that works for YOU. It must feel right for YOU to work and be successful.

Some people jump out of bed and are awake and ready to go. For others, it takes a few moments to fully wake and get started on their day. Work with whatever comes naturally. For me, rising at around 8:00 or 9:00 am is optimal. I have my daily routine before I leave my bedroom/bathroom and making my bed is key to that daily routine. It does two things for me—it enables me to feel accomplished first thing in the morning by completing a very specific task and it brings a sense of calm knowing that when I leave that space, things are in order. And I get more awake as my body moves and expels some energy. As a result, I start my day in a positive mode, feeling like I am in control, organized, and focused.

When I learned about Admiral William H. McRaven's book, *Make Your Bed: Little Things That Can Change Your Life,* I was intrigued due to my own routine and the power I knew it held. In his book, Admiral McRaven shares principles he learned during Navy SEAL training and included in a commencement speech at the University of Texas at Austin on May 17, 2014: "If you want to change the world, start off by making your bed." In his book, he talks about how performing this one constant act each day is mental preparation for how the rest of the day will go. It shows discipline, attention to detail, and leaves one with a sense of pride no matter how small the task, first thing in the morning. It enables you to start your day in a positive direction. One task completed and completed well. The power in this one action is huge. Now, if I begin my day without making my bed, I feel off, like my day will not be as organized or directed. This concept has immense mental impact.

I also find that when I really need to focus on a task that is tedious or requires my attention for a significant period of time, it is helpful to make a cup of coffee or tea. Something about the ritual of having a cup of coffee or tea makes the task more palatable.

How can you create a successful routine?

1. Take the time to think about your day and your week, your activities and what you want to accomplish. You may have a job that demands a certain number of hours per day or family members who require attention at certain times during the day. You might want

to add in some exercise time or time to work on a special project or goal. Take a high-level look at what is flexible, what isn't, and get a visual understanding of what a typical day and week look like. Your routine may be different on different days—that's okay. It's whatever you set up as the routine.

2. Think about who you are as a person, when you are most productive, and what you need to be engaged, focused, and successful in accomplishing your goals. For instance, if you are not an early riser and have a really hard time getting up and functioning before 8:00 am, then setting up an exercise routine first thing in the morning will not work for you no matter how hard you try. It's like swimming upstream. Be realistic. Better to try and work with what comes naturally.

3. Give yourself time and recognize that new habits aren't created overnight. Some habits are easier to form than others, and some people may find it easier to develop new behaviors. There's no right or wrong timeline. The only timeline that matters is the one that works best for you. Your brain likes habits because they're efficient. When you automate common actions, you free up mental resources for other tasks.

4. Focus on the result and why you are trying to establish this routine. The most important thing is to start small and just get started. Consistency is more important than what you accomplish each time. Keep things simple and easy to follow. Remember the old adage from the story of the tortoise and the hare: "Slow and steady wins the race." Once you feel the momentum, it will carry you forward. And we talked a bit before about

finding someone who is supportive in your life. This would be a great opportunity for that person to check in and see how you are doing and provide encouragement.

5. Be flexible. Things will come up that interrupt your plans. Just stay strong, regroup, and try again. Tomorrow is a new day.

A big part of creating new habits or routines is being mindful or aware of what you are doing. We will go into more detail on this topic in Chapter 6, Success Mindsets. The point is, **set yourself up for success**. Find what works for YOU. It must feel right for YOU to work and be successful.

Routine Exercise Example

Here is an example of my weekly routine.

MON	TUES	WED	THURS	FRI	SAT	SUN
Rise 8 am	Rise 8 am	Rise 8 am	Rise 8 am	Rise 8 am	Rise 9 am (extra rest)	Rise 9 am (extra rest)
Exercise	Job	Exercise	Job	Grocery Shopping	Work Toward Goal	Personal Tasks
Prepare Lunch	Lunch Leftovers	Prepare Lunch	Lunch-on-the-Go	Prepare Lunch	Prepare Lunch	Prepare Lunch
Job	Job	Job	Job	Personal Tasks	Visit Parent	Personal Tasks
Prepare Dinner	Other family members cook & cleanup to provide extra time	Left-over Night	Prepare Dinner	Exercise	Exercise	Prepare Dinner / Weekly Food Prep
Plan Forward	Work Toward Goal	**Plan Forward**	Job	Take-out or Left-over Night	**Plan Forward**	**Plan Forward**
Relax/ Read 8-10 pm	**Plan Forward**	Relax/ Read 8-10 pm	**Plan Forward**	**Plan Forward**	Date Night	Relax/ Read 8-10 pm
Bedtime 11 pm	Bedtime 11 pm	Bedtime 11 pm	Bedtime 11 pm	Bedtime 11 pm	Bedtime 11 pm	Bedtime 11 pm

My weekly routine...

➤ Creates a wake-up and bedtime routine—very import-ant to feeling good and having energy.

➤ Incorporates exercise four times per week—time that I have identified as most important to my health and well- being.

➤ Considers my home responsibilities, including check-ing in with an elderly parent.

➤ Builds in some additional time via food preparation and cleanup assistance.

➤ Allows additional rest time, which I need from time to time.

➤ Creates special time with my spouse.

➤ Provides time for me to work on tasks that map to the goals I have identified as things I would like to accomplish.

Note: This routine is a guideline. Some days I will need to work late and will not have time to relax and read before bedtime. Some weeks I must rise early for appointments or flex the day that I visit with my mother. Again, this is a guideline to help you create a routine that is realistic and unique to you.

Take a moment now to think about what a daily and weekly routine looks like for you. Think about your daily and weekly activities and responsibilities and what you want to accomplish. Give thought to who you are as a person and what will set you up for success.

Routine Exercise Template

MON	TUES	WED	THURS	FRI	SAT	SUN

Next: tools. There are some **simple yet powerful tools** you can use to start your day off productively and follow your routine. Let's talk about some of those tools now.

STRATEGY 4

Utilize Tools

"A good tool improves the way you work. A great tool improves the way you think."

– Jeff Duntemann

THIS CHAPTER IS DESIGNED to provide you with some simple yet powerful tools that you can use to stay on task and accomplish your goals. Planners typically manage hundreds of tasks across many categories with varying target dates, all of which must fit together to result in a successful event at the appropriate time. To manage larger, more complex projects, planners typically use more complicated tools. However, for everyday life, we want to keep things as quick and easy as possible. Tools should enhance the planning process and help make your life easier. And tools don't need to be complicated to be effective. Don't underestimate the power of simple tools.

1. Lists

Let's talk about lists. There is power in making lists and crossing off things when they are complete. There is a sense of accomplishment, and this is very important in helping you to feel that you are moving plans forward. Lists also allow you to pivot as necessary and keep track of where you left off, a very important productivity skill.

I remember years ago having a conversation with a colleague about how to stay on task and was shocked when this individual said, "I guess I should make a list. I don't really do that." What? I thought...doesn't everyone make lists? How else could you remember what to do?

I live by lists. Lists enable me to let go, knowing that I won't forget the information that is floating around in my mind. If I don't write things down, I feel scattered, unorganized, and unable to focus. With a list, I can just follow along and not stop to think about what is coming next. The key is to separate the "thinking" phase from the "doing" phase so that, in the moment, you can focus on the tasks at hand.

Let's look at a sample task list. I believe in keeping tools simple and easy, nothing complicated. In the examples below, I have used Microsoft Excel because I am familiar with this program and it gives me ultimate flexibility. But you can use Google Sheets or some other list application. Microsoft To Do is a cloud-based task management application that allows users to manage tasks from a smartphone, tablet, and computer. It is super easy to use and if you are already using Microsoft Calendar, you can easily drag and drop tasks to create calendar entries, a very handy feature.

My list includes things I want to remember as far out as necessary. In this example, I have included the day of the week in addition to the date. You don't have to list the day of the week unless that information is helpful to you. I have included it here as I find it helpful to know the day of the week when assigning dates to tasks.

You can also map to your values or goals if you find that helpful. I have elected not to add my values and goals to my task list as, on a daily basis, I like to keep things as simple and streamlined as possible and I feel that posting my Value/Goal list where I can view it daily is sufficient for me to ensure my task list is staying on target. But this book is about what works for you, so by all means, create a format that supports your success.

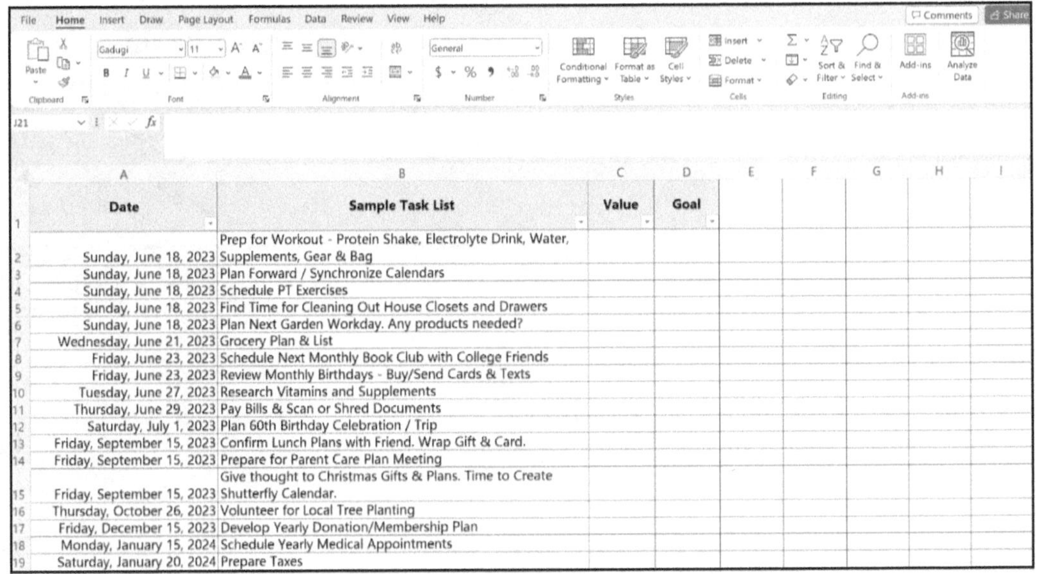

By adding a filter, I can sort my list by date so that the most urgent tasks appear first. I can then easily move tasks around by changing the date and re-sorting the list. If I add other columns, I can sort by those items as well.

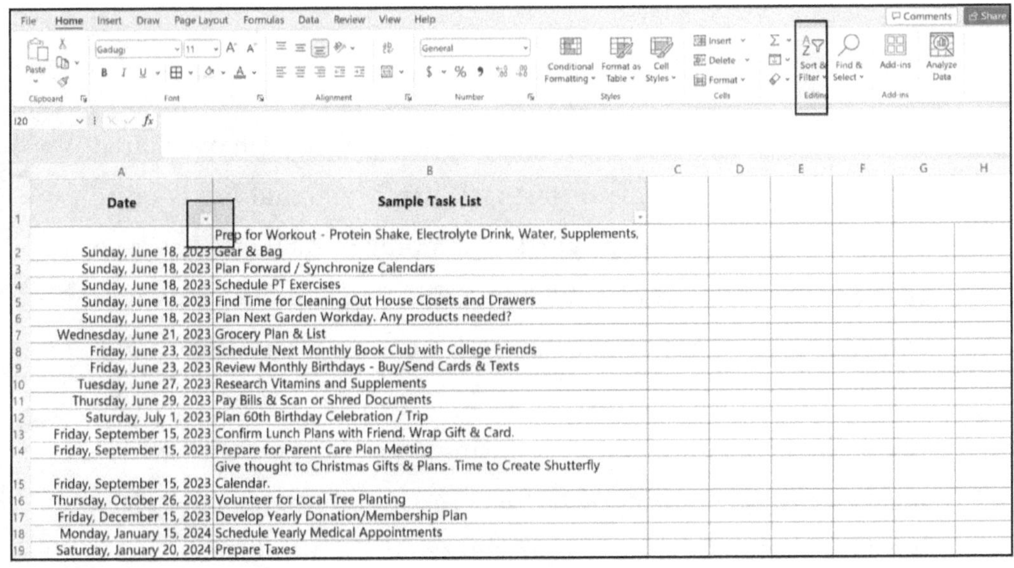

If a particular task requires many subtasks, you can create a separate spreadsheet that you can refer to when you have time to devote to that task or create a separate tab in the "Task List" spreadsheet—whatever works best for you.

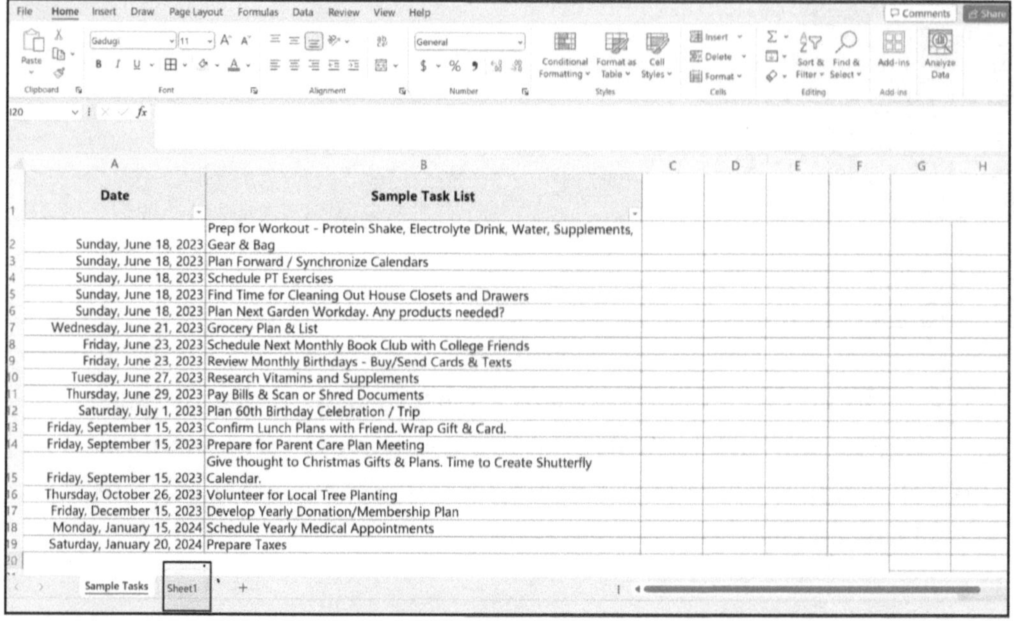

Date	Sample Task List
Sunday, June 18, 2023	Prep for Workout - Protein Shake, Electrolyte Drink, Water, Supplements, Gear & Bag
Sunday, June 18, 2023	Plan Forward / Synchronize Calendars
Sunday, June 18, 2023	Schedule PT Exercises
Sunday, June 18, 2023	Find Time for Cleaning Out House Closets and Drawers
Sunday, June 18, 2023	Plan Next Garden Workday. Any products needed?
Wednesday, June 21, 2023	Grocery Plan & List
Friday, June 23, 2023	Schedule Next Monthly Book Club with College Friends
Friday, June 23, 2023	Review Monthly Birthdays - Buy/Send Cards & Texts
Tuesday, June 27, 2023	Research Vitamins and Supplements
Thursday, June 29, 2023	Pay Bills & Scan or Shred Documents
Saturday, July 1, 2023	Plan 60th Birthday Celebration / Trip
Friday, September 15, 2023	Confirm Lunch Plans with Friend. Wrap Gift & Card.
Friday, September 15, 2023	Prepare for Parent Care Plan Meeting
Friday, September 15, 2023	Give thought to Christmas Gifts & Plans. Time to Create Shutterfly Calendar.
Thursday, October 26, 2023	Volunteer for Local Tree Planting
Friday, December 15, 2023	Develop Yearly Donation/Membership Plan
Monday, January 15, 2024	Schedule Yearly Medical Appointments
Saturday, January 20, 2024	Prepare Taxes

Don't be worried if your list is very long. What I have shared in this book is a sample of my task list. My actual list is quite long and runs into future years. The point of having a list is so that you can clear your mind, know that you won't forget about something you need to address, and focus on the tasks at hand.

Typically, task lists include some larger, more time-consuming tasks and some easier, less time-consuming tasks, which makes sense given life's activities. In the following example, I have highlighted the tasks that will require a bit of time.

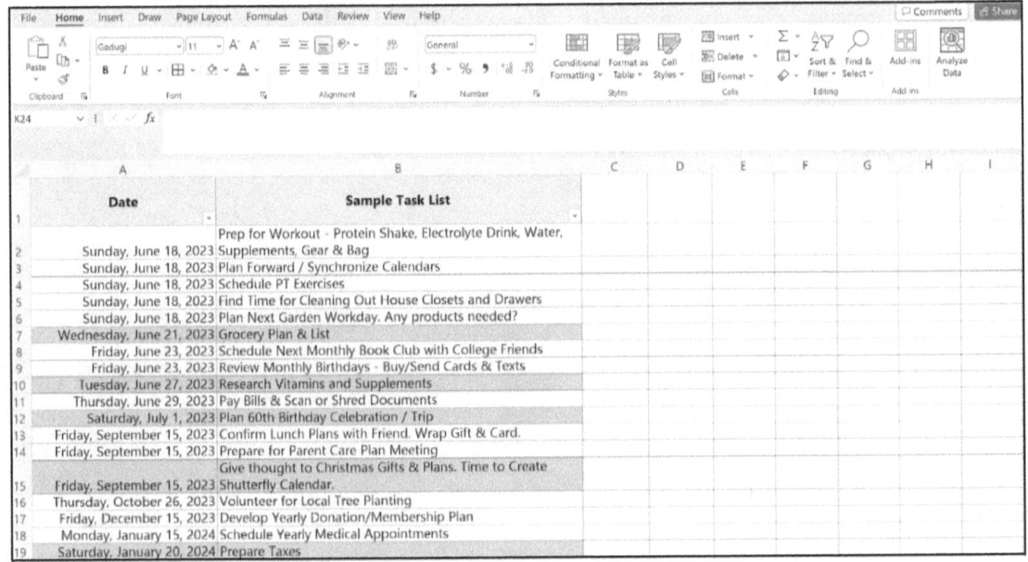

Date	Sample Task List
Sunday, June 18, 2023	Prep for Workout - Protein Shake, Electrolyte Drink, Water, Supplements, Gear & Bag
Sunday, June 18, 2023	Plan Forward / Synchronize Calendars
Sunday, June 18, 2023	Schedule PT Exercises
Sunday, June 18, 2023	Find Time for Cleaning Out House Closets and Drawers
Sunday, June 18, 2023	Plan Next Garden Workday. Any products needed?
Wednesday, June 21, 2023	Grocery Plan & List
Friday, June 23, 2023	Schedule Next Monthly Book Club with College Friends
Friday, June 23, 2023	Review Monthly Birthdays - Buy/Send Cards & Texts
Tuesday, June 27, 2023	Research Vitamins and Supplements
Thursday, June 29, 2023	Pay Bills & Scan or Shred Documents
Saturday, July 1, 2023	Plan 60th Birthday Celebration / Trip
Friday, September 15, 2023	Confirm Lunch Plans with Friend. Wrap Gift & Card.
Friday, September 15, 2023	Prepare for Parent Care Plan Meeting
Friday, September 15, 2023	Give thought to Christmas Gifts & Plans. Time to Create Shutterfly Calendar.
Thursday, October 26, 2023	Volunteer for Local Tree Planting
Friday, December 15, 2023	Develop Yearly Donation/Membership Plan
Monday, January 15, 2024	Schedule Yearly Medical Appointments
Saturday, January 20, 2024	Prepare Taxes

Each of these tasks might require an hour or more. This is when the use of a calendar, the second tool, becomes extremely important. You need to understand how much time you have and how much time you can devote to certain tasks on a given day. Even if you only have half an hour, that focused attention will move a task forward and gradually, little by little, you will accomplish your goals.

2. Calendar

Crucial to the process of planning your time is the second tool: using a calendar. How else can you know how much time you have available to accomplish your goals? It's important to be realistic when entering time in your calendar. If anything, over-estimate the amount of time it will take to complete a task. If you underestimate the time it will take to complete a task, you will only become increasingly frustrated, and this will not set you up for success.

Below is an example of my weekly schedule. As you can see, once you add the details in a visual format, you can easily see how much or how little time you have available in a given day or week.

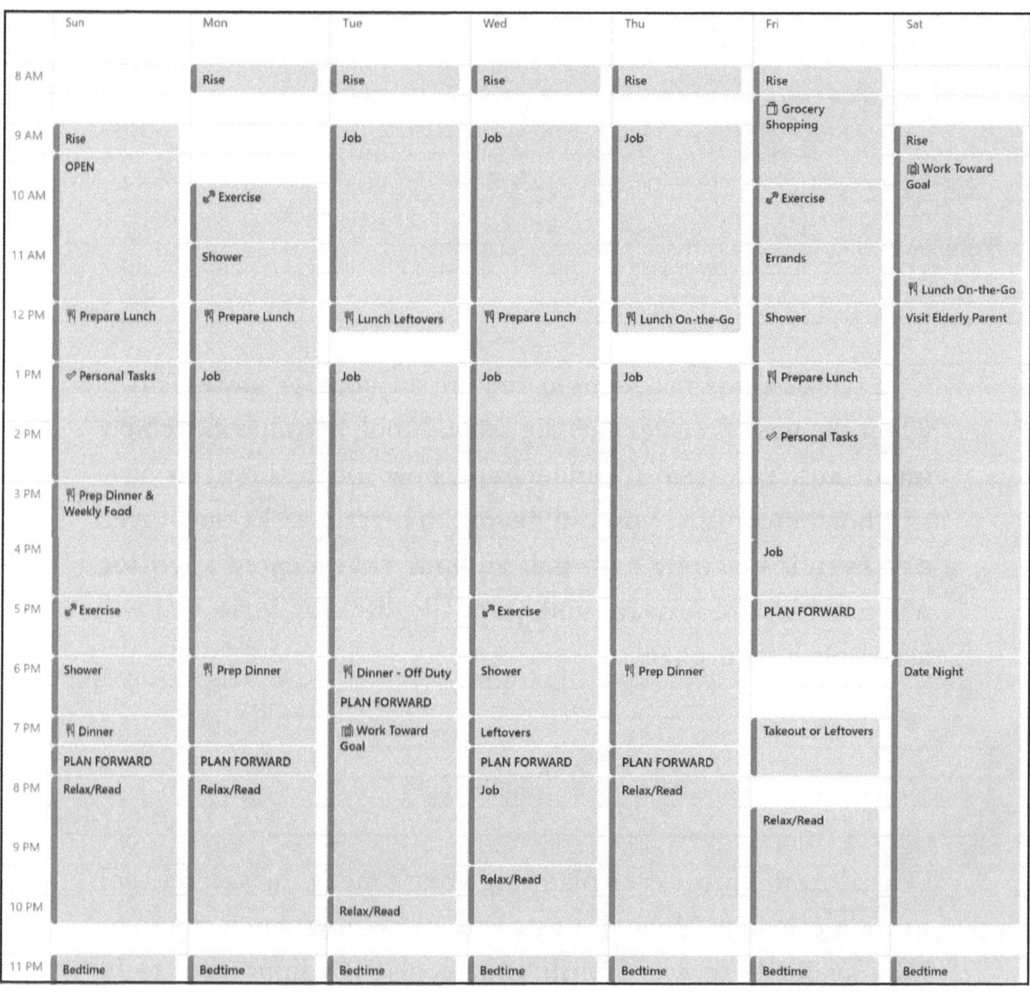

If there are items that repeat each week or follow a specific pattern, set them up as recurring entries to save data entry time. This also enables you to block time for appointments that can't change or prioritize actions where you are trying to create a habit, such as designated exercise time.

I also schedule "free or unstructured" time. It may sound odd, but it's very important. If you don't schedule it, it will never happen. Things <u>will</u> get backed up. You <u>will</u> get behind—it is inevitable. By incorporating free or unstructured time, you give yourself some breathing room. You don't want the process to drive you—you want to drive the process.

The important thing is to make a commitment to yourself. Treat your appointments like business appointments—with respect and as something that can't be changed at the last minute. Make these commitments priorities in your daily routine. And don't be afraid to block your work calendar or close your door if you need to focus. An "Open Door Policy" doesn't mean you need to talk to someone immediately. If it is not a convenient time to talk, tell them that you want to give them your full attention and ask them if they could please request an appointment. Remember, you want to be in control of your time, not the other way around.

There are many calendar applications that you can utilize. I use Microsoft Outlook Calendar. Select the one that works best for you.

3. Timers

The third tool I use routinely is a timer. I set timers throughout my day for key tasks and events so I can let go of "worry thoughts" and focus on the task at hand, knowing that I won't forget to take care of something else at the appropriate time. In today's world, our brains are overloaded—we can't possibly manage it all without some assistance. You can also use timers to keep you on task when you have more than one thing to accomplish. It is a great way to keep things moving along by devoting a designated amount of time to one task before moving on to another. Timers are a simple but very powerful tool.

Okay, you've identified your goals, obstacles, routine, and tools. Now, let's see how everything works together with the **power of a plan.**

STRATEGY 5

Embrace the Power of a Plan

"For tomorrow belongs to the people who prepare
for it today."

– African Proverb

ONE OF MY FAVORITE mantras is "It takes time to make time." It takes time to develop a plan. But having a plan is like having a superpower. Once you have it, it's just a matter of execution, which to me is much easier. With a plan, you are less likely to get sidetracked. With a plan, you have a goal in mind and steps to get there. You just need to follow along. Having a plan is the difference between action and inaction. And having a plan is helpful no matter the task or goal size. The process is the same.

A crucial part of the planning process is what I call **"Planning Forward."** This process involves thinking broadly as well as keeping track of the details. At the beginning of each week, I spend time looking at what is coming up, what is on my task list, and what my priorities need to be that week. This gives me a sense of what I realistically will be able to accomplish that week. The key here is being realistic. If you don't take time for this process, you'll think you can accomplish way more than you actually can, which is not setting yourself up for success. Instead, you'll be in a constant state of frustration trying to move things forward but being unable to do so. If your deadline is defined and can't be moved, such as an event, then you'll also want to **"Work Backward"** by giving thought to certain tasks that MUST be accomplished by a certain date and ensuring these tasks receive priority.

Remember earlier when we talked about separating the "thinking" phase from the "doing" phase? This is the thinking phase and is necessary to master your schedule and work your plan.

The Process

Step 1

At the end of each day, I review my task list, cross off any tasks that I completed, and "plan forward" any remaining tasks. I do this by adjusting the dates on my task list and re-sorting the list. For tasks that are completed, I add a date in the future, like 12/31/2029, and when the list is re-sorted, those tasks will automatically go to the bottom of the list where they can be deleted. For tasks that I do daily, I move them to the next day. If you are using Microsoft To Do, you can mark these tasks as completed and then remove them if you wish or simply delete them from your task list immediately.

Step 2

Once I have removed any completed tasks from my list and moved daily tasks forward, I then address other tasks that were on my list but not accomplished and access my calendar. At this point, I need to look at the time I have available for the next day and the entire week and determine if, in fact, I can devote the time necessary to accomplish certain tasks. If not, I will need to "Move Forward" some tasks to another day. If you don't know an exact date at this point when you will be able to address a particular task, simply move the task forward to a week or month when you think you will have more time and you can re-visit that task at that time. The exact time doesn't need to be identified now. The important point is that you won't lose track of tasks that you are not able to address immediately.

Once you give this thought, re-sort the list again. Follow this process until you have identified your list for the next day.

Step 3

At this point, I update my calendar to reflect my plan. I block out time to address the tasks that I have identified. This keeps my plan realistic and enables me to "follow along" and be more productive. I also number my tasks in priority order so that I address the most important tasks first. That way, if my day doesn't turn out as planned and I am only able to accomplish one task, at least it is the one that I deem most important, and I address that task at a time during the day when I am most effective. See how this all fits together?

The convenient thing about using integrated applications like Microsoft Outlook Calendar and To Do is that you can drag and drop a task into your calendar to create a calendar entry very easily. With Microsoft To Do, you can also select the "star icon" to mark tasks as important and sort those tasks to group them together. A program like Microsoft Excel allows more flexibility in setting up a task list that is unique to your needs and can be easily printed. So, each platform or application has its pros and cons. You'll need to determine what works best for you.

Step 4

Finally, I set timers on my phone for key meetings, appointments, or tasks that must be accomplished the next day. Again, this enables me to focus on the task at hand knowing that I won't forget to switch tasks when appropriate.

Step 5

On Sundays, I follow this same process, but I look at my calendar for the week and make any adjustments to my time as necessary. Perhaps an event or appointment was added to your schedule or perhaps you are not feeling well and need to create some extra space. Taking the time to think about your time brings awareness to the moment and lets you know realistically what you will be able to accomplish. This is a big part of setting yourself up for success. And when I feel I need to plan a bit further out to ensure I am meeting my goals, I'll look at my calendar three months in advance, remove or "opt out" of any activities that do not align with my goals, pencil in time to devote to my goals, and reset my direction.

On average, I spend about 20-30 minutes each day reviewing my plan. It may feel counterproductive to spend time "planning forward" when there is so much to do. But it's quite the opposite. If you look realistically at the time that you have available, planning and prioritization help you take control of your schedule, remain focused, and be more successful.

Now it's your turn to develop your process and create a plan that will help you make things happen.

My Plan Exercise Template

Create Your Task List

Once you have identified the application that you will use, create your task list and sort by date. Add categories if that is helpful to you. Review your list alongside your calendar. Think about the general timing of when you would like to accomplish certain goals and block time on your calendar. At this stage, you are working "big picture"—giving thought to your time over the coming weeks and months in order to identify timing and create a plan. The day-to-day process of managing your tasks and calendar will be more immediate.

DUE DATE	TASK	VALUE	GOAL
		63	
DUE DATE	TASK	VALUE	GOAL

Create Your Calendar

Using your calendar tool, block out committed time and "pencil in" time to devote to your goals and related tasks. Each week will look different. If you have tasks or appointments that repeat on a weekly or daily basis, you can add these items as "recurring" to save time. Mapping task timing to your calendar gives you a clear visual image of just how much time you have available to devote to things outside your daily acts of living or responsibilities. It is a real eye-opener! But this process is critical to stopping the feeling of "multitasking and accomplishing nothing."

Some may ask, "Why not just add tasks to a calendar? Why do I need to keep a separate list?" For me, my tasks are too many to manage with only a calendar. I find it easier to maintain a master list of tasks I need and would like to accomplish and then add those items to my calendar as I have time. I use my calendar for appointments and schedule task time around appointments. But if you are at a point in life where you don't have a lot of responsibilities or demands on your time, then perhaps working with only a calendar will work for you. The point is to use tools that help you be more productive and set you up for success.

	MON	TUES	WED	THURS	FRI	SAT	SUN
6:00 am							
7:00 am							
8:00 am							
9:00 am							
10:00 am							
11:00 am							
12:00 pm							
1:00 pm							
2:00 pm							
3:00 pm							
4:00 pm							
5:00 pm							
6:00 pm							
7:00 pm							
8:00 pm							
9:00 pm							
10:00 pm							
11:00 pm							

Work Your Plan

Now that you have your plan, apply the tools we've discussed to "work your plan." At the beginning of each week, look at your calendar for that week and see if anything has changed. Do the same thing each evening. Adjust your task list and calendar as needed based upon any life events that have come your way. Move tasks forward if necessary, prioritize tasks, and set daily timers. By having a plan, you will be able to simply follow along, remain focused, avoid getting distracted, and accomplish your goals.

Now you have your plan. Let's look at the final strategy, **success mindsets**, which will help set you up for long-term success.

STRATEGY 6

Adopt Success Mindsets

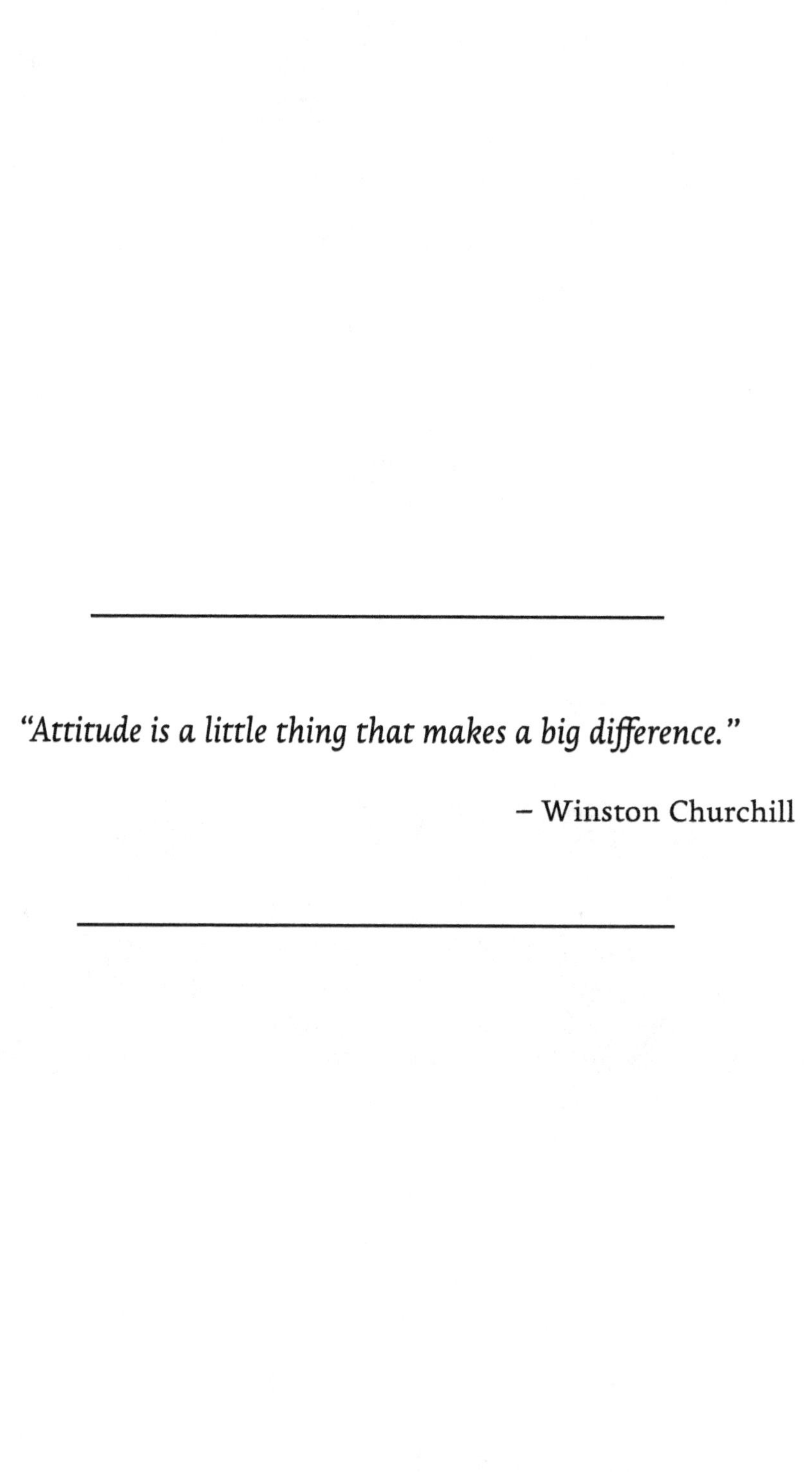

"Attitude is a little thing that makes a big difference."

– Winston Churchill

CONGRATULATIONS! You should feel proud of the steps you have taken thus far to develop a plan, increase your productivity, and accomplish your goals.

While strategies and tools are key components of the planning process, I believe that adopting certain mindsets can work to your advantage and set you up for long-term success. Because let's face it, life can get crazy and there will be ups and downs—that is inevitable—but the mindsets we adopt can have a profound impact on our life experiences and successes.

Mindsets are powerful because they determine how we see the world around us and how we respond, especially in the face of adversity. They can lead us in a positive direction or keep us stuck in old ways. They can make us resilient or give into fear. They can support us in our endeavors or they can undermine us by questioning our resolve.

In my experience, I have found the following mindsets to be essential for success.

EMBRACE CHANGE

"The secret of change is to focus all of your energy not on fighting the old, but on building the new."

– Socrates

One thing is certain: life is constantly changing. And as much as we would like things to remain the same because that brings familiarity and comfort, that is just not realistic. Eventually, all things change. While we can't change this fact, we can change our attitude toward it. Responding to change takes a lot of energy. So the question is, do we want to spend our time and energy fighting the old, or building the new?

There have been many times when I have faced difficult decisions and could have limited myself due to fear and anxiety. I have had to talk with myself to understand the emotions behind my feelings and not give in to the negativity. I think it helps to know that we all have these feelings and that they are totally normal. In fact, it is well documented that the fear response we feel when we are facing change or a difficult situation is part of human evolution. The so-called "fight or flight" response was critical to our survival and still helps us today to avoid dangerous situations, for instance. But we can change our belief in and relationship with stress and use it to our advantage.

According to Andrew Huberman, neuroscientist, associate professor of neurobiology at Stanford University School of Medicine, and host of the Huberman Lab Podcast, how we think about stress impacts the stress response in profound ways. Learning that stress is a way of mobilizing resources in the body can work to our advantage. Obviously, if we are under extreme, prolonged stress such as dealing with a debilitating illness, this is a different situation. But knowing that, with greater awareness and understanding of what is happening, we can modify our response to stress is powerful.

I completely understand the challenges associated with being outside your comfort zone because I have a very active fight-or-flight response in certain situations. For instance, I am afraid of heights and so anytime I am in an elevated state—whether in the balcony of a theater or driving up a mountain or climbing a narrow stairwell or skiing above tree line—I feel a very intense fight-or-flight reaction: my heart starts to pound, I get extremely nervous, and I start to shake. It can be debilitating. But avoiding these activities would mean that I would miss out on so many wonderful experiences and things I love to do, like going to the theater and being in the mountains and skiing.

I have also helped my aging parents downsize several times and relocate my son to Colorado—talk about a lot of change. It's a lot to absorb—not only the physical aspects of moving, but the emotional aspects as well. I tried to focus on my gratitude for the opportunity to help my parents transition to a new stage in life and be their advocate as well as spend precious one-on-one time with my son driving cross-country in his car. These activities have brought me much joy and contentment.

It truly is our attitude and perspective toward something that matters most. Sometimes simply accepting the situation can be a good place to start.

Think about a time when you've been faced with change—how you've felt about it and how you've handled it. Maybe you needed to change jobs, move to a new community, or assist an elderly parent with relocation. Maybe a change has been thrust upon you, outside of your control. Maybe you recently married or had a child.

Change can be scary. It can be stressful. And fear can keep us stuck in place. But change can also be exhilarating. It's our response to it that can make all the difference. Ask yourself, "How can I look at this differently?" "What's the worst that can happen?" "What is the silver lining?" By opening ourselves to new thoughts and possibilities, we can achieve incredible results.

PRACTICE AWARENESS

"Awareness isn't passive. It directly leads to action (or inaction)."

– Deepak Chopra

You have probably noticed that being realistic is a key theme throughout this book. Being realistic is a big part of the planning process and to be realistic, you need to be aware. Without awareness, change is not possible. You need to understand what is happening around you and what is realistic to accomplish. Say no to some things and not to others. Realize when your mind is wandering and you need to bring it back into focus. Or realize that today is an "off" day and you need to move on from a particular task. Everyone's mind wanders. However, awareness helps you identify what is happening and adjust accordingly. You can have all the tools at your fingertips, but without awareness, you will not be able to plan effectively.

One of the most well-known voices on awareness and self-realization is Deepak Chopra, founder of the Chopra Foundation and a world-renowned pioneer in integrative medicine and personal transformation. In his studies of alternative medicine and wellness, Deepak Chopra believes that the way forward when you feel stuck, numb, frustrated, and stymied is to address your state of awareness. "What refuses to move must be shown how to move. Because pure awareness lies at the basis of everything, the most powerful way to change your life is to begin with your awareness. When your consciousness changes, your situation will change."

I describe awareness as watching yourself "move through the world" and observing your actions in real-time. It's sort of like watching yourself in a movie. Seeing the consequences your actions are having on yourself, others, and the world around you is a necessary step in creating change.

For instance, if we want to improve our health, then we need to monitor and adjust our eating and exercise habits. If we want to develop strong friendships, then we need to invest the time and effort in planning get-togethers and staying in touch. And if we want to become better parents, then we need to research and apply good parenting skills in our lives. It's the same in all aspects of our lives, including our productivity. Awareness allows us to be "in the moment," understand what is happening around us, and make changes to improve our situation.

Paying attention to how you move in the world can be life changing. So, give yourself the gift of awareness. Watch yourself move through your day and bring greater awareness to your actions. Observe yourself in action, "in the moment." Ask yourself, "How am I feeling?" "What change is necessary?" "Am I presenting positive or negative energy?" "Why is this situation presenting itself?" "What am I to learn?" "Can I do this a different way?"

This information will be immensely helpful as you better understand yourself, work your plan, and accomplish your goals.

EXHIBIT DISCIPLINE & CONSISTENCY

"Success isn't overnight. It's when every day you get a little better than before. It adds up."

– Dwayne "The Rock" Johnson

To me, discipline and consistency are essential for setting yourself up for success. To be good at something, you need the discipline to work at it and practice it, and you need to do that consistently over time. Discipline and consistency are behind just about every successful process. Even creative professionals, such as painters, artists, dancers, writers, etc., utilize discipline and consistency in some fashion, whether it be in a daily routine, a format that is used, or a process that is followed.

Sometimes it is hard to get started or to have the discipline required to stay on course. The key to success is to start small but be consistent. Simply one hour a week toward a new goal can be transformative. It's not about how much you accomplish each time. It's about getting started and establishing a habit. It does not happen overnight. But once you feel success, it will build momentum.

I have seen this in my own life, in particular with my exercise and nutrition routine. Some days it is hard to find the motivation to do what I know will result in the best outcome. But then I think of how I feel when I exhibit the discipline to exercise consistently and eat healthy. I feel stronger, healthier, empowered. I feel more energetic and focused and, as a result, more productive. Tapping into those feelings gives me the incentive to continue and reinforces a positive outcome.

Think about the discipline and consistency required by a professional athlete. When asked, most athletes would tell you that success didn't happen overnight, but rather step by step with effort, discipline, and consistency. The way to get better at something is to practice it over and over. Dealing with our daily responsibilities is no different. We can improve our productivity and accomplish our goals if we have a plan and work at it.

Start by implementing a task every day, like making your bed or some other task that you identify. This will make you feel empowered and set you up for success. The important thing is to develop a plan that works for you and then follow that plan. Start small but be consistent, and please be kind to yourself in this process. Realize that change is not easy, but it is doable. It will not be perfect every day. Getting started is what matters. You are capable of doing anything you set your mind to—it just takes some discipline and consistency.

BELIEVE IN YOURSELF

"If you don't believe in yourself then why is anyone else going to?"

– Tom Brady

Finally, believe in yourself. You've got this! It's not complicated. It's just a bit of organization and a shift in mindsets—all totally doable. One of the most important things you can do for yourself is surround yourself with positive people. Even ONE person can make a difference. We ALL need encouragement. The key is to identify YOUR "cheerleader"—someone with whom you can share your goals and call for support when things get off track. This is important because we all have positive voices and negative voices that speak to us, and sometimes the negative voices take over. Having someone who can reinforce your positive voice and provide encouragement in those moments of doubt can make a world of difference.

Maybe it is a best friend.

Maybe it is your spouse.

Maybe it is a minister or professional therapist.

Believe me, I can be my own worst critic. The voice that sits on my left shoulder can sometimes be the loudest. That's why this step is so important.

And by the way, it is also totally fine to talk to yourself—in your mind or out loud if necessary (although you might raise some eyebrows from those around you). You are not losing your mind. In fact, this is a great way to keep on task as long as your "brain talk" is positive, kind, and helpful. I routinely tell myself, in my head, "Okay, Melissa. You've got this. Just sit down, take charge, and get it done." A totally harmless practice that creates positive results. I especially use this in times when I am trying to overcome anxiety brought on by fear of the unknown, and it works wonders.

One of the things that helps me stay motivated is to post inspiring quotes in places where I can reference them daily. I've included some of my favorite quotes throughout this book. This last quote was given to me by a very dear friend who is one of my cheerleaders. She has been my friend through ups and downs, crazy ideas, and fun adventures, and has always been there to support me and believe in me, even when I didn't believe in myself. She was instrumental in me accomplishing my dream of writing this book, and I think of her every time I read this quote. Perhaps you will find it inspiring too.

"Your time is limited, so don't waste it living someone else's life. Don't be trapped by dogma—which is living with the results of other people's thinking. Don't let the noise of other's opinions drown out your own inner voice. And most important, have the courage to follow your heart and intuition. They somehow already know what you truly want to become. Everything else is secondary."

– Steve Jobs

CONCLUSION

I hope you have found the simple strategies and insights in this book helpful for accomplishing your goals.

➢ **Focus** is critical to staying on task and driving plans forward.

➢ **Visualization** is powerful in keeping your goals in front of you daily.

➢ **Overcoming obstacles** is necessary to remove distractions that are holding you back from realizing success.

➢ **Establishing a routine** creates discipline, which is necessary for accomplishing any goal. And this must be unique to you to be effective.

➢ **Simple tools** can be powerful. You do not need to overcomplicate the process to be effective.

➢ Creating a plan takes time up front, but **working your plan** is the key to maintaining focus and keeping you from feeling overwhelmed.

➢ Having tools and strategies will only get you so far. **Building success mindsets** is essential for long-term success.

Taking just one action can make a profound difference. So, I'll leave you with this worksheet to help you get started immediately. By following this list of actions, you'll be on your way to think like a planner and make things happen in your life. I believe in you. Good luck!

Think Like a Planner Worksheet

1. Create **one** visual of your goals that you can reference daily to stay focused.

2. Identify at least **one** task that doesn't support your goals and let it go.

3. Identify **one** way to eliminate obstacles.

4. Identify **one** way to add structure to your daily routine **that works for <u>you</u>**.

5. Identify **one** application that you can use to organize your tasks.

6. Identify **one** 20-30-minute time block at the end of each day to "plan forward."

7. Identify **one** way to practice awareness daily.

8. Identify **one** task that will allow you to practice discipline and consistency daily.

9. Identify at least **one** person who can be your "cheerleader."

10. Identify **one** inspiring quote that you reference daily to stay motivated.

RESOURCES

The Rough Guide to Psychology, An Introduction to Human Behavior and the Mind, Dr. Christian Jarrett.

Manage Your Day-to-Day: Build Your Routine, Find Your Focus, and Sharpen Your Creative Mind, Jocelyn K. Glei.

Blog in HuffPost, formerly the Huffington Post: *The Science of Visualization: Maximizing Your Brain's Potential During the Recession*, Srinivasan Pillay, CEO of NeuroBusiness Group and award-winning author.

CNBC, *SCIENCE OF SUCCESS: Do this for 5 minutes every day to rewire your brain for success, according to neuroscience*, Kabir Sehgal and Deepak Chopra.

Atomic Habits: An Easy & Proven Way to Build Good Habits & Break Bad Ones, James Clear.

Dare to Lead Values List, Brene Brown.

Attention Span, A Groundbreaking Way to Restore Balance, Happiness and Productivity, Gloria Mark, Ph.D.

Make Your Bed: Little Things That Can Change Your Life, Admiral William H. McRaven.

The Huberman Lab Podcast, Dr. Andrew Huberman, neuroscientist and associate professor of neurobiology at Stanford University School of Medicine.

Levels of Awareness, Deepak Chopra, MD, FACP, CRCP, founder of the Chopra Foundation and a world-renowned pioneer in integrative medicine and personal transformation.

EXERCISE TEMPLATES & WORKSHEET

Reference these templates and worksheet as you develop your unique plan.

Core Values Exercise

Refer to the values list you have identified and list the **five (5) values** that describe or resonate with you the most.

Core Values Exercise Template

My five (5) core values. Feel free to add more if necessary.

1.

2.

3.

4.

5.

Goals Exercise

Take a moment to give thought to your goals and assign a time frame for each.

Goals Exercise Template

Identify three (3) goals & time frames.

Goal:

Time Frame:

Goal:

Time Frame:

Goal:

Time Frame:

Visual Plan Exercise

Create a visual plan. Print it out and post it where you can see it daily as a reminder of what you deem most important and what you intend to accomplish.

Visual Plan Exercise Template

GOALS	VALUE	TIME FRAME
1.		
2.		
3.		

Obstacle Exercise

Identify **three (3) obstacles** that create distraction and ways to let them go. Add more if necessary.

Obstacle Exercise Template

OBSTACLE	RESOLUTION
1.	
2.	
3.	
4.	
5.	

Routine Exercise

Take a moment to think about your daily and weekly activities and responsibilities and what you want to accomplish. Give thought to who you are as a person and what will set you up for success.

Routine Exercise Template

	MON	TUES	WED	THURS	FRI	SAT	SUN
Morning							
Afternoon							
Evening							

Create Your Task List

Use your tool of choice to create your task list.

Task List Exercise Template

DUE DATE	TASK	VALUE	GOAL

Create Your Calendar

Use your tool of choice to create your calendar.

Calendar Exercise Template

	MON	TUES	WED	THURS	FRI	SAT	SUN
6:00 am							
7:00 am							
8:00 am							
9:00 am							
10:00 am							
11:00 am							
12:00 pm							
1:00 pm							
2:00 pm							
3:00 pm							
4:00 pm							
5:00 pm							
6:00 pm							
7:00 pm							
8:00 pm							
9:00 pm							
10:00 pm							
11:00 pm							

Think Like a Planner Worksheet

Taking action builds confidence and puts you on a path to achieve your goals. Follow this list of actions to think like a planner, set yourself up for success, and make things happen in your life.

1. Create **one** visual of your goals that you can reference daily to stay focused.

2. Identify at least **one** task that doesn't support your goals and let it go.

3. Identify **one** way to eliminate obstacles.

4. Identify **one** way to add structure to your daily routine **that works for <u>you</u>.**

5. Identify **one** application that you can use to organize your tasks.

6. Identify **one** 20-30-minute time block at the end of each day to "plan forward."

7. Identify **one** way to practice awareness daily.

8. Identify **one** task that will allow you to practice discipline and consistency daily.

9. Identify at least **one** person who can be your "cheerleader."

10. Identify **one** inspiring quote that you reference daily to stay motivated.

ACKNOWLEDGMENTS

To my family and friends who believed in me and encouraged me—thank you. Your love and support mean the world to me.

To the Atmosphere Press team who helped me overcome obstacles and make this book a reality—thank you. I am forever grateful that the universe brought me to your doorstep and encouraged me to walk through.

To my son Adam, of whom I am immensely proud—may you be inspired to work hard, believe in yourself, and follow your dreams. It's never too late to make things happen!

ABOUT ATMOSPHERE PRESS

Founded in 2015, Atmosphere Press was built on the principles of Honesty, Transparency, Professionalism, Kindness, and Making Your Book Awesome. As an ethical and author-friendly hybrid press, we stay true to that founding mission today.

If you're a reader, enter our giveaway for a free book here:

SCAN TO ENTER
BOOK GIVEAWAY

If you're a writer, submit your manuscript for consideration here:

SCAN TO SUBMIT
MANUSCRIPT

And always feel free to visit Atmosphere Press and our authors online at atmospherepress.com. See you there soon!

ABOUT THE AUTHOR

MELISSA DELMONEGO has been a corporate event planner for more than thirty years. She has an unwavering passion for organizing and leading projects to successful completion. Now, Melissa shares her expertise and productivity techniques outside the corporate arena so that others can experience a greater sense of accomplishment in their daily lives.

Melissa was born in Gettysburg, Pennsylvania. She has a Business Degree in Marketing and Management from Susquehanna University. When not working, Melissa enjoys planning trips and sharing new adventures with her family. Her happy place is in the mountains. Favorite activities include skiing, fitness training, hiking, writing, cooking, and being in nature. Melissa resides with her husband in Chester Springs, Pennsylvania.

You can visit Melissa's website at
www.thinklikeaplanner.com